Wholesome

Wholesome Eats

36 Original Recipes created for
your good health and enjoyment

By

Jill Etheridge

ASPECT

Wholesome Eats
Jill Etheridge

Published by Aspect Design 2012
Malvern, Worcestershire, United Kingdom.

Designed, printed and bound by Aspect Design
89 Newtown Road, Malvern, Worcs. WR14 1PD
United Kingdom
Tel: 01684 561567
E-mail: allan@aspect-design.net
Website: www.aspect-design.net

A copy of this book has been deposited with the British Library Board

ISBN 978-1-908832-22-1

Acknowledgements

The first person I wish to thank is my lovely husband David Etheridge for all the encouragement he has given me as I have created these recipes over several years, not least because he's the one who's tasted them all and given me marks out of ten for each one! His help has also been invaluable in the final stages of preparation for the book.

My daughter Vanessa and sons Zuhayr and Steven inspired me to enjoy cooking even more as they grew up, and grand-daughter Amy gets her own mention in a recipe for a very special cake.

My photographer Jane Horton showed vast amounts of patience in the Etheridge kitchen while we set up tempting displays of fresh ingredients to go with some of the recipes. We hope you love the results as much as we do. As she said, as a duo we were doing what would normally take a whole team of stylists etc.

Thanks to Dr Rosy Daniel for my Mentor Training with Health Creation and for the fact that that inspired all this.

Finally I'd like to thank Allan at Aspect for his calm and clear advice as the book was prepared for publication and Paul for all his work on it.

Deep appreciation and gratitude to you all.

Jill Etheridge
November 2012

Contents

Before you start cooking...

The inspiration for this collection of original recipes came while I was training to be a Health Creation Mentor. The Health Creation Programme has a number of very helpful pages which guide the reader on how best to eat to sustain or regain good health.

At home, I had already been including 'Five a day' of fruit and vegetables in my eating for many many years, long before the magazines and supermarkets started to advocate this. I had cut my dairy food intake to very little indeed, finding lifelong catarrhal conditions much improved by this, and learning over the years that a number of illnesses seem to be linked to excessive dairy food consumption.

Similarly I came to understand that obesity and diabetes are by no means the only health problems caused by the vast amounts of sugar that the average person in the UK and the US tends to eat. I soon found – as you will see when you come to the recipes for cakes and puddings – that there is so much wonderful natural sweetness in fruit and some nuts that we really do not need sucrose at all, especially not refined white sugar.

I should make it clear that I am not a Nutritionist. There are many good books and practitioners who can give you detailed advice if you have specialised requirements. It's also true to say that, in my many years as a Natural Therapist, I have discovered that opinions among my colleagues varied widely as to what constitutes 'healthy eating'.

There is no shortage of information elsewhere about, for instance, which types of fat are compatible with healthy eating, and which are definitely unhealthy. I will outline below the criteria which guided the development of the recipes.

With the exception of one, they are all Vegetarian, and the only one with meat has a vegetarian version. They are all high in vegetable or fruit content and low in fat, keeping off saturated fat with the exception of the ones containing creamed coconut. There is a view that, because this is of plant origin, it is not harmful in the same way as animal-origin saturated fat. Various pulses and nuts provide the necessary protein.

The amount of dairy ingredients is minuscule and can easily be omitted if, for example, a topping includes a small amount of grated Italian hard cheese. In the one or two recipes where a little additional sweetness seems necessary, a small amount of fructose is used, and in one case runny honey.

In an ideal world, we would always use fresh, local organic ingredients in season. This is a counsel of perfection that, for various reasons, we can't all attain. Many of us are short of time and shop to a tight budget. So tinned tomatoes are often mentioned, rather than fresh. The choice is yours.

Cooking methods are important to health. There is some frying, but in just a little oil, often with a splash of water and a lid on, and never in order to turn the food dark brown. Grilling, likewise, is light. Nowhere will you see a microwave oven mentioned! But there is a piece of modern equipment which I heartily recommend, and which takes away all excuses that it's too time-consuming to cook from scratch; that is a food processor. When my trusty one broke, I got a brand-new boxed one from a cash converter shop – an unwanted wedding present, no doubt.

Happy cooking, and may your health and well-being flourish!

Jill Etheridge

Main Courses

Contents

Main Courses

Aubergine and Chick Pea Bake

Preparation: 20 minutes
ADVANCE COOKING OF CHICK PEAS RECOMMENDED
Cooking: 30–35 minutes total
Serves: 3–4

Soak one mugful of **Chick Peas** in a basin overnight, or for a couple of hours, drain, bring to the boil in fresh water, throw away first water, then add fresh and cook for about 40 minutes, until they are easy to bite into. (Or use a can of chick peas!) Wash and slice 2 large **Aubergines** in rounds. Pour a little **Olive Oil** onto a baking tray, arrange aubergine slices, then turn them over, adding a little more oil if needed to ensure every slice is lightly coated.

Bake in the oven at 220°C / 200°C Fan / Mark 7 for 12–15 minutes (or under high grill, until brown each side).

Meanwhile slice 1 medium **onion** and soak in enough boiling water to cover. (This makes them much less likely to repeat on you.) Slice 3 sticks **celery**, then drain and rinse the onion and 'steam-fry' it with the celery for 7–8 minutes: i.e. put just a little oil in a small frying pan and cook over a low heat keeping the lid on tightly.

Open a tin of **Chopped Tomatoes** and put half of them in the base of a lasagne dish. Season lightly, then sprinkle with dried Oregano. Add half the Chick Peas and half the Aubergine slices. Next spread the Onion and Celery over, then the rest of the Tomatoes and Chick Peas. For the top layer mix 5–6 tablespoons **Plain Soya 'Yoghurt'** with a generous tablespoon of **Pesto**. Arrange the remaining Aubergine slices, spread the Pesto and 'Yoghurt' mixture over and finally sprinkle with **grated Italian hard cheese** (the dry ready-grated variety is fine).

Bake for 15–20 minutes at 220°C / 200°C Fan / Mark 7 until thoroughly heated through.

Autumn Lasagne

Preparation: 30 minutes
Cooking: 40 minutes total
Serves: 4

This can be served at any season, but with its lovely rich colour combination it reminds me of golden days.

Peel a medium-sized **Butternut Squash** and cut into cubes of about 3cm / 1" – easier to peel if you cut slices, then halve them first. Slice one small **Leek** into rounds. In a large frying pan soften for a few minutes 3–4 sheets of **Lasagne Verde** (depending on the size of your dish) in a little water to which a few drops of oil have been added. Leaving the water in the pan, place the softened sheets in the bottom of the dish, then put the leek and squash into the bottom of the pan and sit another 3–4 sheets of lasagne on top. Simmer with the lid on for 4–5 minutes.

Drain a tin of **Plum Tomatoes** and reserve the juice. *Put half the leek and butternut squash, half the tomatoes (each one snipped into 3–4 pieces, according to size) and half a packet of **Firm Silken Tofu** cut into cubes onto the bottom layer. Season to taste, sprinkling over a couple of pinches of dried thyme.* Add the next layer of softened lasagne sheets and immediately put a third and final batch in the pan to soften, ensuring there's enough water left in the pan. *Repeat from * to **

Heat the oven to 200°C / 180°C Fan / Mark 6. Mix one heaped dessertspoon of **Potato** (or **Corn**) **Flour**, one dessertspoon of **Garlic Purée**, one teaspoon each of **Dijon Mustard** and **Wholegrain Mustard** and the reserved tomato juice in a small basin or large cup. Mix thoroughly and pour over the layers, helping it to soak through. Now add the third (top) layer of lasagne sheets. In the same basin, blend together half of a 200g tub of **Hummus** and a little **Soya** or other non-dairy milk. Top the lasagne with this then sprinkle the crumbs made from one thick slice of **Wholemeal Bread**. (Roughly rubbed over a grater will do.) Heat thoroughly in the oven for about 25 minutes until lightly browned.

Brown Lentil and Aubergine Medley

Preparation: 30 minutes
Cooking: 40 minutes total
Serves: 2–3

Put 125 g / 4 oz **Brown** or **Green Lentils** in a pan and cover with three times their volume of boiling water. Lay 2 sprigs of **Rosemary** on top and cover the pan loosely with a lid. Cook for 25–30 minutes till tender but not mushy. While they are cooking wash and slice 1 yellow **Courgette**, then wash 1 large **Aubergine** and cut it into 4 thick slices down the length. Place about 2 tablespoons of **Olive Oil** in the bottom of a clean grill pan and arrange these sliced vegetables in a single layer. Cook them under a medium heat grill for 5 minutes each side, until they are lightly golden.

Leaving the slices to cool a little, now wash 1 small head of **Broccoli** dividing it into tiny florets a little bigger than your thumbnail, with the stalks not too long. I also use a bit of the upper end of the stalk cut very thinly, and any excess length from the floret stems. Now wash 1 stick of **Celery** and peel and grate 1 medium-sized raw **Beetroot**. (You can then join the Red Hand Gang!)

Before draining the lentils, carefully save the fallen strands of rosemary and discard the stems. In a food processor whizz the slightly cooled aubergine with the rosemary and the celery stick – roughly cut up first – but keep the courgette slices out as they need simply to be quartered. Boil the kettle and, when all other preparations have been completed, pour enough boiling water to cover the broccoli in a large pan. Let it steep for about 5 minutes while you warm a serving dish. Now boil it for just 1 minute, drain and add all the other ingredients, except the grated beetroot. Warm all through thoroughly, stirring gently,then just before serving add the beetroot and about 6 Chives snipped small.

Cassoulet-style Layer with Two Potato Mash

(Needs hob and grill only)

Preparation: 25 minutes
Cooking: 25 minutes
Serves: 2–3

Cook 4 **meat-free Sausages** (preferably by grilling), according to the directions on the pack. When cooked cut each into 4 pieces. While they are cooking peel one **Cooking Apple**, 3 medium-sized **Sweet Potatoes** and scrub or peel 3 **ordinary potatoes**. Cut all in chunks and boil ordinary potatoes only for 5 minutes. Now add the sweet potatoes and cook both types for 8 minutes. Finally add the chunks of cooking apple and cook for only about 2–3 minutes, watching that the apple doesn't overcook, or it will mix with the water.

While these are cooking peel and cube 2 rings of **Butternut Squash** from the wider end, about 2 cm / 1" thick, and wash and slice half a **Leek** finely and 2 sticks of **Celery**. Sauté these three together in a little **Sunflower Oil**, with a lid on the pan, for about 8 minutes. Then add to the pan ½ tin of **Chopped Tomatoes** and one drained tin of **Mixed Beans** (canned in water, not vinaigrette!). Warm all through gently with 2–3 pinches of **Mixed Herbs** until thoroughly hot.

Warm a lasagne dish with the potato water and mash the potatoes and apple mix with a little olive oil . Empty the water out of the dish, pour in the sausage and vegetable mix and top with the mash. Sprinkle over 2 tablespoons fresh **wholemeal breadcrumbs** mixed with a little dried **grated Italian Cheese**. Brown under a medium grill, watching carefully, until the crumbs are golden brown.

Chick Pea Rissoles

Preparation: 20 minutes
Cooking: 20 minutes
Serves: 3–4

Now there's a word you don't hear much these days; Mother always made them with the left overs of the Sunday (meat!) joint. Call these 'burgers' if you will; but I won't!

In a food processor chop finely 1 small **Onion**. Fry it gently in a little **Sunflower Oil**, in a large frying pan. Drain 1 can of **Chick Peas** and put in food processor with one and a half washed, cored and quartered **Eating Apples** (not too sweet a variety), 1 **Egg**, a pinch each of dried **Thyme**, **Cumin** and **Coriander**, 1–2 teaspoons each of **Garlic Purée** and **Vegetable Purée**, with seasoning to taste. Add in the cooked onion and combine all together.

Heat a little oil in the frying pan used for the onions, ensuring none of them are stuck to pan. The chick pea mixture should be slightly firm, but not dry. If not firm enough, whizz in a little **Gram Flour** (made from chick peas.) Spoon 8–9 dollops into the hot pan, patting them with the back of the spoon into rissole shapes. Fry over medium heat for about 8–10 minutes, turning half way.

While the rissoles are cooking, whizz in a blender 1 large Carrot (peeled and roughly chunked) with half a carton of **Passata***. Stir in 1 dessertspoon **Potato** (or **Corn**) **Flour**, mix in thoroughly with a few drops of Worcestershire or genuine **Soy Sauce** if liked then heat gently and serve as a sauce.

** If you need to avoid Tomatoes, use two handfuls of fresh Rocket or Baby Spinach instead of the Passata.*

Courgette, Leek and Bean Pasta Bake

Preparation: 10–15 minutes
Cooking: 25–30 minutes total
Serves: 2

Wash and slice thinly 1 medium-sized **Leek**, and wash and chop one small **Red Pepper**, if liked. Fry gently in a little **Olive Oil**, to which a splash of hot water has been added, with a lid on the frying pan.

Meanwhile cut 1 medium-sized **Courgette** in four along the length (crossways); then, holding all together, cut thick slices across. Add these to the pan with 1–2 crushed cloves of **garlic** (or 10 cm / 6" from a tube of Garlic Purée). Stir together and replace the lid.

Now put 2 mugfuls of **Wholewheat Pasta** to cook in boiling salted water for the recommended time on the packet. While it is cooking season the vegetable mix to taste, then add 1 teaspoon dried **Thyme** (or leaves of 2–3 stems fresh if available) and 1 can of **Mixed Beans** drained.

Cook gently with the lid on for 8–10 minutes, stirring from time to time. Drain the pasta. In a lasagne dish put half the bean and vegetable mix, then half the pasta, then the same again. Top with a light scattering of grated **Leicester Cheese** and 1 tablespoon of grated **Parmesan** or equivalent (heaped if fresh, level if dried). Heat through at 220°C / 200°C Fan / Mark 7 for 10–15 minutes, until the cheese is melted and lightly browned.

Crunchy-topped Celeriac and Chick Peas

Preparation: 25 minutes
Cooking: 20 minutes total
Serves: 2–3

Peel and cut half a medium **Celeriac** into chunks. Boil in a little water for 8–10 minutes. Peel 1 large **Carrot** and set aside.

Slice 1 **Leek** finely, or chop in processor. In a large stainless frying pan gently heat one dessertspoon of **Sunflower Oil**, add the sliced leek, followed by a splash of boiling water, then immediately put the lid on tightly. Cook for 5 minutes.

Chop together in a processor 2 tablespoons of **Cashew Nuts** and one thick slice of **Granary Bread** for the final topping.

Drain the celeriac when cooked. Open one 400g tin of **Chick Peas** and add these to the cooked leek. Stir well together with one heaped teaspoon of **Wholegrain Mustard** and a teaspoonful of **Dried Thyme**. Tip the mixture into a warm lasagne dish, or similar.

Light a grill on medium heat and keep the dish of vegetables warm. As quickly as possible whizz in a liquidiser the carrot, 300 ml of not quite boiling water or stock, and a handful of washed fresh **Coriander**. Pour over the mixture, top with the nuts and crumbs and grill gently until piping hot and lightly browned.

Haricots Florentine with Tangy Mash

Preparation: 25 minutes
Cooking: 25 minutes
Serves: 2–3

Peel 500g (1 lb) **Old Potatoes**, cut into chunks and give them a 10 minute head start boiling in a large pan. Meanwhile peel 200g (1 medium) **Sweet Potato** and cut it into slices 1cm (½") thick. Next peel 1 large **Cooking Apple** and slice thickly into a bowl of lightly salted water to keep it from turning brown. Now peel and slice 1 medium **Onion**, then wash and chop half a small **Green Pepper** and half a small **Yellow Pepper**. As soon as the ordinary potatoes have had their first 10 minutes, add the sweet potato slices and set a timer for 5 minutes. At the end of that time drain off most of the water and add the sliced cooking apple for 2–3 minutes, until soft. (You don't want to lose the apple flavour into the full amount of cooking water that will be drained off.) Drain the remaining water as soon as the apple is softened.

In an ordinary saucepan pour a little **Sunflower Oil** and sweat the sliced onion and sweet peppers with half a bag of **Baby Leaf Spinach**, until the leaves are just wilted. (Alternatively use 6–8 lumps of Frozen Spinach, and heat with the onion, breaking up the lumps as they thaw, and allowing all the water to evaporate quickly as soon as the lumps are thawed.) Add 1 tin drained **Haricots**, 1 tin of **Chopped Tomatoes** with their juice and a teaspoon of **Nutmeg**. Put a heatproof shallow dish to warm under a low grill. When the spinach/tomato/chick peas are all thoroughly heated together, stir in 100 g (a good 3 oz) of **Hummus** and now warm very gently.

Mash the potatoes and apple and put on top of the pan mixture after transferring it to the warmed dish. Drizzle with a little Olive Oil and sizzle under the grill until piping hot.

Herby Breakfast-for-Supper

Preparation: 15 minutes
Cooking: 35 minutes total
Serves: 2–3

This recipe shouldn't really be here at all, but my husband David, who has had all these recipes tested on him, and gives me marks out of ten, gave this ***A TEN!*** *I call it a* ***Bridge*** *recipe.... because if you want to start eating healthier food, not all the household is likely to be equally enthusiastic. With a few 'bridge' recipes, where you add some healthy new items while still leaving familiar well-loved ingredients in for now, there may be more willingness to try new tastes.*

Scrub 4 fairly large **old Potatoes**, slice them about ½ cm (¼") thick and put in a pan of water to boil for about 12 minutes. You want them tender, but not breaking up. Chop a small **Onion** and cook in a frying pan until very lightly browned. Remove the rind and all the fat under it from a 250g pack of lean **Back Bacon**.* (Vege version below) Now remove the onion from the pan so you can heat the rashers in a single layer until they turn pink, doing the same for both sides.

Oil a lasagne dish, or similar, put ⅓ of the cooked potato slices in the bottom, then scatter half the onion over. Snip half the bacon rashers into pieces and scatter these also, as well as half a tinful of **Chopped Tomatoes** in Juice. Beat together 2 **Eggs** and pour half of the mixture over the bottom layer. Season with a little freshly-milled black pepper and a pinch each of **dried Basil** and dried **Oregano**. Now repeat the layer exactly as the first time, again using just a third of the potato slices.

Finally stir a little **Olive Oil** into 100g **Hummus** (half a smaller tub.) Put the remaining ⅓ of the potato slices onto the layers and spread the hummus mix as a topping. Place in the oven at 220°C / 200° C Fan / Mark 7 for 20 minutes,until golden.

* *VARIATION You can make the bottom layer* ***Chopped Frozen Spinach*** *with half a* ***Leek*** *finely sliced and softened and use ½ tin of* ***Borlotti Beans*** *in place of half the bacon, or a whole tin if omitting bacon.*

Instant Chick Pea and Tomato Supper

Only needs hob.

Preparation: 10 minutes
Cooking: 15 minutes
Serves: 2

(Well, almost instant....!)

Wash carefully and slice thinly 1 **Leek**, then fry it over a medium heat in **Olive Oil**, with a splash of water, in a lidded saucepan. After about 5 minutes leave the lid off and turn the heat up a little to let the steam evaporate and the leek go golden.

Keeping your eye on the leeks, boil a kettle and prepare a bowl by warming it first with hot water. Fill a half pint mug up to ⅔ full with **Wholewheat Couscous** and then add **Quinoa** to level the mix up to the top. Tip into the bowl, cover with boiling water or veg stock, season to taste (a little lemon or lime juice adds a good tang), stir well and cover, leaving it to stand for 10 minutes. (Some packets recommend cooking the couscous and/or quinoa in a pan, so follow directions.)

Now add to the leeks 1 tin of **Chopped Tomatoes** with juice and 1 tin of drained **Chick Peas**, 1 teaspoon each of **Ground Coriander**, **Cumin** and **Dried Thyme**. Stir well, heat through thoroughly and serve with the couscous and quinoa mix.

> **Note:** *The flavour of Quinoa can take some getting used to, but it really is a great nutrient, high in protein and low in calories. By mixing it in with the couscous and serving it with a tasty vegetable and pulse mix you get a very wholesome meal!*

Lentil and Tomato Savoury

Preparation: 10 minutes
Cooking: 25–30 minutes
Serves: 2–3

Peel and slice 1 **Onion**, placing it in a pan with 100 g / 3½ oz **Red Lentils** and 200 ml / 7 fl oz **water** or **stock** and the **juice** from a tin of **Chopped Tomatoes**. Bring to the boil carefully, then simmer gently with a lid on, timed carefully for 5 minutes, then simmer without the lid for a further 5 minutes to allow the surplus liquid to evaporate. Add the tomatoes, a teaspoon each of **dried Basil** and **Oregano**, 1 teaspoon made **English Mustard**, 50 g / scant 2 oz grated **Leicester Cheese** and 1 tablespoon (about 7 g) of grated **Italian Cheese**. (I use vacuum-packed grated Grana Padarno from one of the cheaper supermarkets. Once opened, I keep it in the freezer so it keeps thoroughly fresh however slowly I use it.)

If you want to keep dairy-free, try mashing down a pack of silken tofu in place of the cheeses and add an extra teaspoonful of made mustard for more flavour.

Leave mixture to cool a little and warm through a suitable dish under a low grill or in the oven. After lentil mixture has cooled for about 3 minutes, carefully stir in 100 ml / 3–4 fl oz **Soya Milk** and 1 beaten **Egg**. Adjust seasoning, then pour into the warmed dish and top with just a small scattering of grated Leicester Cheese, or with a few wholemeal breadcrumbs. (I keep some of each always to hand in the freezer to save time.) Brown under a low grill for 10–15 minutes until golden, or in the oven at 220°C / 200°C Fan Oven / Mark 7 for the same time.

This is delicious served with a Jacket Potato and green salad.

Mixed Mash Garden Veg Cottage Pie

Preparation: 20 minutes
Cooking: 30–35 minutes
Serves: 2

Scrub one very large **Potato** and peel one medium-sized **Parsnip** and cut them into large chunks. Wash and cut into chunks 2 **Eating Apples** (*or*, if preferred, for a sharper flavour, one large **Cooking Apple**, which may need peeling if tough-skinned). Boil all these together for about 15 minutes, or until easy to mash. Wash and chop finely 3 sticks **Celery**, then scrub or peel 1 large **Carrot** and grate it. Wash and chop a handful of **Fresh Coriander**. (A Food Processor would make light of all this chopping/grating if you prefer.) Place a tinful of **Mixed Beans** and its liquor (*be sure to buy the type with no sugar added*) in the base of a warmed ovenproof dish, then add the chopped celery, carrot and coriander. Drain the potato mixture and mash, adding a good teaspoon of dried **Thyme** or **Sage**, seasoning to taste, and a dessertspoonful of **Wholegrain Mustard** if liked. Spread over the veg, drizzle with **Olive Oil** and heat through in the oven at 200°C / 180°C Fan / Mark 6 for 15 minutes, until piping hot.

Note: *It is unusual to have virtually raw veg in the base of a pie, but this way you get all the freshness of the flavours, and the crunch of the celery contrasts deliciously with the smooth texture of the mash.*

Nutty Stuffed Courgettes

Please note that people who don't like nuts will probably not even be aware of them in this. You could try!

Preparation: 20 minutes
Cooking: 30 minutes
Serves: 3

This is best prepared in a Food Processor, and really quick to do in that way.

Wash 3 fairly fat **Courgettes** (*or* 1 medium **Marrow**). Slice a fairly shallow 'lid' off the courgettes, then scoop out the centre flesh. (Keep, if courgettes; discard if marrow.) Now boil a little water, and in a small basin place 2 tablespoons **Quinoa** and 2 teaspoons **mild curry powder**. Add just enough boiling water to cover and leave to soak.

In the food processor,whizz ½ a peeled medium-sized **Onion** till finely chopped, then add 1 cup **Cashew Nuts** and ⅓ cup **Almonds** and whizz again till very finely ground. Next add 1 washed or peeled **Carrot** and half a **Sweet Potato** in chunks, at the same time adding 1 dessertspoon **Garlic Purée**, 2 tablespoons **Tomato Purée**, 1 teaspoon each of dried **Marjoram** and **Thyme**. Add the soaked quinoa and 4 tablespoons **Porridge Oats**. Season to taste, if necessary, Whizz again till thoroughly blended, then use to stuff the courgettes. replace 'lids' and place on a baking tray.

Bake them at 180°C / 160°C Fan / Mark 4 for 30 minutes until tender, and filling piping hot. Marrow will take 45–50 minutes.

Pasta Shell Bake

Preparation: 30 minutes
Cooking: 20 minutes if grilled, 30 minutes if baked
Serves: 2–3

Dice half a peeled **Butternut Squash** and 125 g (4 oz) **Celeriac**, then slice half a **Leek**. Simmer these in a medium-sized pan, in just enough water to cover, for 10–12 minutes until just softened. In a larger pan, bring lightly salted water to boil and add one mugful of **Wholewheat Pasta Shells** (or similar), cooking according to the directions on the packet.

Meanwhile empty 1 tin **Chopped Tomatoes** into a Lasagne dish. Season if required and sprinkle with a few pinches of **Dried Herbs** as preferred (e.g. **Basil, Oregano**). On top of the tomatoes place *EITHER* 1 can **Borlotti Beans**, drained, *OR* 1 pack **Tofu**, cubed. Warm all these through in the oven at 180°C / 160°C Fan / Mark 4, covered with tinfoil loosely on top. When the vegetables in the pan are cooked, drain these, reserving the stock, (you will need the pan again), and place them as the next layer in the lasagne dish, returning it to the oven, again covered.

In a large cup blend 1 heaped teaspoon of **Potato** (or **Corn**) **Flour** in a little cold water, then add the slightly cooled stock left when you drained the vegetables. Keep this to one side. Drain the pasta and tip it onto the tomato bean and vegetable mix.

Now stir the potato flour and stock mix thoroughly again and return it to the empty veg pan. Bring slowly to the boil, stirring carefully all the time and making sure to have a little extra cold water nearby in case the 'glaze' is too thick. Once it's a suitable consistency pour over the pasta, sprinkle with 60 g (2 oz) grated **Parmesan Cheese**. (Use less if it's sold dried in a tub.) Pop under the grill for a minute or two to brown slightly, or in oven at 220°C / 200°C Fan / Mark 7.

Red Kidney Bean Risotto

Preparation: 20 minutes
Cooking: 30–40 minutes
Serves: 4

Wash and slice thinly ½ a **Leek** and 2 sticks **Celery**. Wash or wipe 3 open cap **Mushrooms** and break or cut them into small chunks. Cut one thick slice off the wide end of a **Butternut Squash**, peel it and then cut into small cubes, sugar lump size, then wash half a **Red Pepper** and cut into chunks.

In a large frying pan (you will need a lid for it later) gently fry the vegetables in a little **Sunflower Oil** until lightly browned, stirring from time to time. Now add 225 g / 8 oz. **Arborio Rice**, (or **Brown Basmati** if you prefer the wholegrain to the authentic Italian touch!) with just the **juice** from a tin of **Chopped Tomatoes** made up to 550 ml / 1 pt with water or vegetable stock.

Note: *If you are able to find short wholegrain rice to use it is best to soak it overnight.*

When the rice is almost cooked (check packet as cooking times vary) add the **Chopped Tomatoes** and a drained canful of **Red Kidney Beans** together with a good shake of good quality **Soy Sauce** and 1 teaspoon of **Dried Thyme**. Heat all through until piping hot, keeping the lid on and stirring occasionally.

Spinach and Potato Layer

Preparation: 20–25 minutes.
Cooking: 30 minutes total.
Serves: 2–3

Scrub and slice 4 medium **Potatoes**, about 5mm / ¼" thick. If liked, add a few slices of **Celeriac** for extra flavour.

Peel and slice 1 medium **Onion**. Boil the potato, onion and celeriac gently for 10 minutes. Reserve the cooking liquid.

Put a layer of half the potatoes etc. in the bottom of a lasagne dish, or similar. Season as desired, then add 1 bag **Spinach leaves** roughly torn, spice with a good sprinkling of **ground Nutmeg**, scatter over 2 handfuls of **Cashew Nuts***/**, then 2 (of 3) **fresh Tomatoes** (sliced) and season, adding 10–12 torn-up **Basil leaves**.

**(If desired, the Cashew Nuts can be lightly toasted under a grill or gently dry-fried in a dry non-stick frying pan to develop the flavour, and a light brown colour).*

Now add a top layer of the remaining potato mixture. Mix one heaped tablespoonful of **Hummus** with one cupful of the reserved **cooking liquid** and pour evenly over the potato slices. Finally add the third **Tomato**, sliced, and a sprinkling of **Sesame Seeds** and **Sunflower Seeds**.

*** If nuts are to be avoided, or for a change, cook a cupful of* ***Puy Lentils*** *and substitute for the Cashews.*

Bake at 220°C / 200°C Fan / Mark 7 for 15–20 minutes.

Sweet Potato Cakes

A rissole by another name !!

Preparation: 15 minutes
Cooking: 25 minutes
Serves: 3

Peel 1 large **Sweet Potato** and cut into chunks. Boil for about 12 minutes, until soft but not at all mushy. Meanwhile chop 1 small **Onion** and fry gently in a little **Sunflower Oil** in a large frying pan until lightly browned. Assemble the remaining ingredients; then when the sweet potato is cooked, drain it *really well* and mash until smooth. Now add the onions, one heaped teaspoon of **Wholegrain Mustard**, 2 teaspoons of **Garlic Purée**, 2 heaped teaspoons of **Green** *OR* **Red Pesto**, 2 tablespoons **Porridge Oats**, 1 Egg, beaten, a 400g can of **Cannelini** or **Mixed Beans** (*very* well drained of their water). Stir all together until well blended.

Form into about 9 rounds with floured hands, or simply dollop into the onion pan to which a little extra oil has been added. Fry gently for 4 to 5 minutes on each side, until golden brown. These will turn into loosely-formed cakes, which are moist enough not to need a sauce especially.

Serve with a mixed green salad.

Veggie Bolognese Sauce

Hob only required.

Preparation: 10 minutes
Cooking: 30 minutes.
Serves: 2

In a food processor whizz together half a peeled **Onion**, 1 medium-sized peeled **Carrot**, half a washed **Courgette**, 2 chunked scrubbed sticks of **Celery**, 2 cloves of **Garlic** and 1 tablespoon of **Sunflower Seeds**. If using peeled **Tinned Tomatoes** (as opposed to ready-chopped), add these to the bowl now, but keep the juice out at this stage, or it could fly everywhere!

Put the tomato juice in a large saucepan, add the vegetable mix along with a rubbed sprig of **fresh Thyme**, 2 teaspoons **dried Oregano**, ⅔ tin of water (rinsed round the tomato tin) and 2 tablespoons of **Tomato Purée**. Stir well and simmer gently for 15 minutes.

Meanwhile rinse and dry the processor bowl ready to whizz together 100 g / 3 oz **Cashew Nuts** and 100 g / 3 oz mixture of **Almonds**, **Brazils** and **Hazels**, as liked. Chop in the processor until quite fine. When the vegetable mix has had the 15 minute simmer add the nuts and 60 g / 2 oz **Millet Flakes**, season to taste and simmer for another 15 minutes, stirring frequently. During this time put **Spaghetti** or preferred pasta to cook for the required time and drain well before topping with the sauce and sprinkling a little grated **Italian Cheese** if you wish.

Vegetable and Bean Bake topped with Limey Sweet Potato and Couscous

Preparation: 20 minutes
Cooking: 30 minutes total
Serves: 2–3

Boil 2 mugfuls water in a kettle. Peel about 200 g (6 oz) of **Sweet Potato** (two small or one medium). Cut them into 1cm slices and boil gently in a pan in a little of the hot water, for about 10 minutes, or until soft enough to mash, but not mushy. Drain as soon as ready, but keep the lid on. Peel 1 large **Onion** and 2 **Carrots** and slice them thinly. Wash, trim and slice 2 sticks of **Celery**. Put 1 cup of **Wholegrain Couscous** into a bowl, cover with boiling water and leave to soak, covered.

Put 3–4 tablespoons of water in a large frying pan and cook the onion, carrot and celery gently with a lid on for 8–10 minutes, until slightly softened. At the end of this time remove the lid and allow any remaining water to evaporate, then add 1 drained tin of **Lima Beans** and 1 can of **Plum Tomatoes**, first draining but reserving the juice. Heat through thoroughly. Add 1–2 teaspoons of **assorted dried herbs** of your choice (e.g. Basil, Oregano, Marjoram. A few fresh Basil leaves would be even nicer.)

Warm an ovenproof dish in a low oven. Mash the sweet potato, add the soaked couscous, ensuring there is no surplus water in the bottom. Blend together with 1 tablespoon of **Lime Juice** (bottled will do if there's no fresh lime to hand.) Season with freshly-milled black pepper. Pour the beany mix, piping hot, into the dish, top with the couscous mix and pop into the oven at 180°C / 160°C Fan / Mark4, covered with foil, for just 10 minutes, to avoid drying out the couscous. While it is warming through mix 2 heaped teaspoon of **Potato** (or **Corn**) **Flour** with a little water and add to the reserved tomato juice as a sauce, heated in the frying pan used for the veg, stirring all the time as it thickens and adding a little **Pesto** if liked.

Vegetable Moussaka

You really do need a food processor for this recipe.

Preparation: 35 minutes
Cooking: 35 mins total, some during prep time.
Serves: 3–4

Wash 2 large **Aubergines**. Slice one and a half and place them on a baking tray which will fit under the grill and is greased with 2 tablespoons **Olive Oil**. Grill under a high heat, turning once the slices begin to brown, until both sides are golden. Meanwhile peel and quarter 1 large **Onion**, 2 cloves **Garlic** (if liked) and 2 medium-sized **Carrots**. Now wash 1 large **Courgette** and 2 sticks of **Celery**. Cut these into manageable chunks and whizz all the vegetables, except the grilled aubergines, in a food processor with the other half Aubergine.

Warm 2 tablespoons **Oil** in a large frying pan, then gently fry the chopped vegetables with *EITHER* a pack of **Quorn Mince** *OR* 125 g / 4 oz **Chopped Nuts**, stirring as you fry for just about 5 minutes, till everything is lightly coated in the oil.Season to taste including nutmeg. Warm a lasagne dish in the oven, then add 350 ml / generous ½ pint **Passata** to the mixture in the frying pan. Stir thoroughly, then leave to warm through over a very low heat, stirring occasionally while you make the sauce for the topping.

Warm 200 ml **Soya 'Milk'** in a saucepan and as quickly as possible sprinkle on the surface 2 level tablespoons **Wholemeal Flour** and ½ teaspoon **Dry Mustard**, whisking them briskly to disperse. Stir constantly with a wooden spoon until the sauce comes to the boil and allow to cook, still stirring, for 2 minutes. Allow to cool a little, then stir in one beaten **Egg**. Place the frying pan mixture in the warmed dish, top with the grilled aubergine slices and finally top with the sauce and a light scattering of grated tasty **Cheese** (e.g. Leicester). Grill 5–10 minutes at medium heat.

Notes

Puddings and Cakes

Puddings and Cakes

For many years now I've had fresh fruit for 'afters' with my main meal. You can't beat it really, as raw produce maintains all its nutrients, if fresh, and is wonderfully vibrant. An autumn treat is picking blackberries from a safe place, and eating them within minutes, with or without some soya pouring 'cream'. However on Sundays, or if we have guests round for a meal, it makes a nice change to have a pudding; so six recipes are included here.

When a nutritionist recommended many years ago that I needed to completely give up sugar and yeasted products, at least for a good while, that seemed a real challenge. On Sundays I like a cooked lunch and 'bready tea'. So, as you can imagine, I was reluctant to do without a piece of cake. What to do? Well, I set about inventing cakes that relied for sweetness only on the high fruit content. I had already cut out white flour from my baking decades ago, using 100% wholemeal. For the cakes, when a supermarket I used stopped stocking its own brand of self-raising I found that the best results were obtained with Doves Farm brand. We even make our 'Cranks' Christmas Cake sugar-free.

Please note the following points:

- *These cakes are not light and fluffy at all, because of the wholemeal flour and high fruit and often juice content.*
- *With lots of fresh or moist fruit in, they will need to be refrigerated if being kept for a day or two, to prevent mould.*
- *The fact that they have low fat content and low or no added sweetening does not necessarily mean they are low-calorie.*
- *Diabetics should still eat these sugar-free cakes in moderation as they may be high in fruit sugar and starch. If in doubt, show the recipe to your dietician.*

Contents

Puddings

Cakes

Baked Apricot Custard

This is rather like Norwegian Cream, but is dairy-free, and I love it entirely sugar-free.

Preparation: Overnight soak + 5 minutes
Cooking: 1 hr approx
Serves: 3–4

Put about 12 **Dried Apricots** (not ready-to-eat type) in the dish you will bake the custard in and pour over enough boiling water to well cover them. Cover and leave overnight if possible, or at least for several hours. After soaking, drain off as much of the liquid as possible and snip the softened apricots into smallish pieces.

Warm a scant 1 pint of **Rice 'Milk'** in a pan. In a basin, beat together 3 large **Eggs** and just before the 'milk' boils, pour onto the eggs, stirring briskly.

If you are not yet used to very lightly sweetened desserts, you may like to add 1 Dessertspoon ***Fructose****.*

Pour the egg mixture onto the apricots. Sprinkle grated **Nutmeg** over the surface. Place the dish in a larger dish containing cold water so that it comes about half way up the smaller dish. Bake at 180°C / 160°C Fan / Mark 4 for about 1 hour or until firm to the touch. Enjoy hot or cold.

Cranberry and Chocolate Torte

(Wheat-free as well as dairy-free.)
A Christmas-time treat that's only slightly naughty!

Soaking: 2–3 hours, or overnight
Preparation: 35 minutes
Serves: 4–5

Lightly grease a 220 mm / 9" diameter flan dish. Soak half a pack of Fresh or Frozen **Cranberries** in enough **Amaretto liqueur** to cover. (If avoiding alcohol use Red Grape Juice.)

In a 600 ml / pint-sized bowl over, but not touching, hot water (not boiling), melt 100 g **Dairy-free Dark Chocolate** (it should be about 70% cocoa solids). While it is melting, hand crush 4 **Oat Flip biscuits**, or similar. (Check wheat-free recipe if that's important to anyone eating them.)

Once the chocolate has melted, take the basin off the heat, allow to cool slightly then carefully stir in 150 ml / 5 fl oz **Soya pouring 'cream'** (you'll need the rest of the carton for the topping). Now quickly add 2 tablespoons **Ground Almonds**, 1 tablespoon **Hazelnut Meal**, made from toasted hazelnuts, and the crushed oat biscuits. Blend all together thoroughly then spread over the base of the flan dish and leave to set firmly.

Blend together a pack of **Soft Silken Tofu** with the remainder of the carton of **Soya 'Cream'** and 2 tablespoons of **Apple Concentrate**. Once the base is cold and firmly set and the silky topping really smooth, spread this over the base. Just before serving,use a slotted spoon to lift the cranberries out of the liqueur they've soaked in and place them on kitchen paper to blot them. Now spoon them carefully onto the Torte and enjoy!

Note: *This is also good made with raspberries and no liqueur.*

Mango and Coconut Cream

Preparation: 25 minutes
Cooking: None!
Serves: 5–6

With a knife shave a few curls off 1 block **Creamed Coconut** to decorate the dessert before serving. In a saucepan gently melt the rest of it in 200 ml / 6 fl oz **Multi-Fruit Pure Juice.** **see below** (I use one which is called a Multi-Vitamin juice, with 11 different types of fruit juices or purées and carrot, which I buy in one of the cheaper supermarkets. This one has a delicious tang. If preferred, you could use one of the tropical blends, but make sure it is pure juice, no added sugar, and in that case you may like to add a few teaspoons of lime juice for more tang.)

> ***N.B.*** *Once the juice is slightly warmed, be certain to turn off the heat, a) so that the vitamins are not destroyed, and b) so that the coconut does not turn over-thick and cooked.*

Prod the block carefully with the point of a knife to break it up as it melts, and *stir until thoroughly blended* with the juice. (If you are in a hurry, you may like to grate half the block, holding it in its peeled-back inner wrapping, but remember it's greasy, so slippery and rather a messy job!)

Peel and slice 2 **Ripe Mangoes**, which should weigh about 500g / 1 lb in total. **Alternatively** drain 2 tins **Mango.****If it is in natural juice, this should be used as part of the juice the coconut is melted in.** If it is in a light syrup rinse the fruit well. Reserving 3–4 slices for decoration, purée the mangoes in a food processor, then add the melted coconut and juice and blend all together. Pour into a small glass serving bowl, or into individual ramekin dishes, and top with coconut curls and mango slices. Set in a cool place and refrigerate if keeping for a day or two.

This is lovely for a party : simplicity itself!

Pears 'Belle Juliette'

Preparation: 10 minutes
Cooking: 10–15 minutes
Serves: 2

Who, you ask, is Juliette? Well, this recipe is adapted from that for Pears, or rather 'Poires belle Hélène' ...... and I'm not sure if that's named after Helen of Troy, or somebody less famous. I needed to find a different title, so thought I'd Frenchify my name!

In a stainless saucepan warm gently 300 ml / half pint of **Red Grape Juice** with 1 dessertspoon of **sugar-free Blackcurrant Jam**. (I use the French brand in narrow jars.)

Peel and halve two ripish but firm medium-sized **Pears** (I like to choose Rocha or Packham varieties.) Add them to the juice and jam mixture and sprinkle in liberal amounts of cinnamon and/or nutmeg.

Simmer very gently with a lid on for 10–15 minutes, turning them over to ensure all surfaces turn that lovely rich colour.

If you wish, you can slightly thicken the cooking liquid just before serving: remove the pears carefully, allow juice to cool slightly and stir in 1 teaspoon of **Arrowroot** or **Potato** (or **Corn**) **Flour** which has been dissolved in a little cold water. Both of these cook to a pretty clear sauce. Stir very briskly as you add it, as you don't want strings of starch to form. Now warm gently until the sauce is transparent.

Serve with a little **Soya Cream** or **Cashew Nut Cream**, made by whizzing in a liquidiser 60 g / 2 oz **Cashews** with 150 ml / 5 fl oz **Rice 'Milk'**.

Sugar-free Rhubarb Crumble!!

Preparation: 15 minutes
Cooking: 35–40 minutes total
Serves: 4

This is my husband's favourite dessert. After weeks of my making normal ones for him and a sugar-free version for me (I was getting Candida under control) he said he'd happily eat the same as mine, and has loved it ever since! I suggest you get used to low-sugar eating before you try this.

Cut 8 sticks **Rhubarb** into short lengths. Place in a heavy-based pan with a little more than enough sweet **Apple Juice** (non-cloudy) to cover. Wash core and slice 1 large or 2 medium **Dessert Apples** (a fairly sweet variety). Add to the pan and warm slowly over a low heat until it just comes to the boil. Turn heat out and leave lid on tightly while you make the topping.

Blend together 200 g / 6 oz **Wholemeal Plain Flour** with 100 g / 3 oz **Dairy-free Spread** until it resembles coarse breadcrumbs. Now stir in 60 g / 2 oz **Porridge Oats**, 1 teaspoon grated **Nutmeg** and 60 g / 2 oz **Pecan Nuts** roughly crushed between your hands. (If you want to use cashews instead, they will need to be whizzed, as they don't crumble as easily.) These two nuts are sweetish, so – for us – make a perfectly acceptable sugar-free topping. However, if your courage fails you, add a little Fructose into the topping, and maybe into the fruit; but you'll get used to sugar-free in time!

With a slotted spoon, lift the rhubarb and apple pieces into the cooking dish, sprinkle with **Cinnamon** or your preferred spice and top with the crumble mixture. Bake at 190°C / 170°C Fan / Mark 5 for 20–25 minutes, until lightly golden. (Without sugar it doesn't go quite as brown.)

Tutti Frutti Whip

Preparation: 10 minutes
Cooking: None!
Serves: 2

In a food processor bowl, whizz together:

Half a carton of Soft Silken Tofu

1 peeled Kiwi **

½ a peeled Mango

1 small washed unpeeled ripe Pear

1 washed unpeeled Nectarine **

*** reserve one slice of each of these per serving, to decorate. Pour into individual dishes and chill before serving.*

That's it!

Amy's Special Carrot Cake

Preparation: Soaking + 20 minutes
Cooking: 35–40 minutes

This was invented for Amy, one of my lovely grand-daughters. She will eat any amount of fruit, but has made a slow start with vegetables. I wondered if I could adapt my previously favourite Carrot Cake Recipe to take a full pound of carrots! I tried it, and instead of being heavy, it turned out deliciously moist. It definitely has Amy's seal of approval.

Peel 500 g / 1 lb **Carrots** and grate them finely in a food processor. Put 100 g / 3 oz **Sultanas** in a fairly large mixing bowl, then add 3–4 tablespoons of **Honey**, according to desired sweetness, and 50 ml **Lemon Juice** (bottled if no fresh lemons to hand).Now tip in the grated carrots, cover and leave to macerate for an hour or two, if possible. (This plumps up the sultanas wonderfully.)

Add 1 teaspoon each of **Bicarbonate of Soda**, **Grated Nutmeg** and **Ground Cinnamon** to 200 g / 6 oz **Wholemeal Self-Raising Flour**. Add 80 ml / 3 fl oz **Sunflower Oil**, 3 medium or large **Eggs** and the dry goods to the carrot mixture. Stir all thoroughly together and smooth into a lined greased oblong tin approx 20 cm x 30 cm / 8" x 12", or two victoria sandwich tins. Cook at 200°C / 180°C Fan / Mark 5 for 35–40 minutes (oblong tin) and 20–25 minutes in shallow round tins, in all cases until an inserted skewer comes out clean. Allow to stand in tin for 10 minutes, then cool on wire rack.

Optional Frosting: I devised this for a party occasion, and it's simple and scrumptious, setting like a glacé icing, which will crack slightly as you cut it.

Slightly warm 80 ml / 3 fl oz **Carrot Juice** (*OR*, if unobtainable use **Vitamin Juice**), take off heat, stir in 80 g / 3 oz **Creamed Coconut**, breaking it up gently as it softens. Stir till smooth and spread gently over cake once it's cooled. Keep in fridge after day one.

Apricot and Almond Cake

Preparation: Soaking time + 15 minutes
Cooking: 55 minutes

Cut 200 g / 6 oz **Dried Apricots** into 2–3 pieces each and soak them in 150 ml / ¼ pint **Sweet Apple Juice** for 1–2 hours at least. When they are nearly ready mix together 200 g / 6 oz **Dairy-free Spread** suitable for baking, 1–2 oz / 30–60 g **Dark soft brown sugar** (according to taste), 60 g / 2 oz **Ground Almonds**, 30 g / 1 oz **Ground Rice**, 200g / 6oz **Wholemeal Self-Raising Flour**, 2 **Eggs**, 5 ml / 1 teaspoon **Almond Essence** and the soaked apricots.

Turn mixture into a lined greased cake tin (8" diameter) and bake at 190°C / 170°C Fan / Mark 5 for 50–55 minutes, or until a skewer inserted into the middle comes out clean. Allow to cool in the tin.

Apricot and Apple Loaf

Preparation: Soaking time + 15 minutes
Cooking: 45 minutes

Snip 200 g / 6 oz **Dried Apricots** into 3–4 pieces each, then soak them in 200 ml / ⅔ pint sweet **Apple Juice** for 1–2 hours. (If in a hurry, warm the juice first.) Once they are soaked, mix together in a large bowl 100 g / 3 oz **Dairy-Free Spread** (suitable for baking), 250 g / 8 oz **Wholemeal Self-Raising Flour**, 60 g / 2 oz **Ground Hazelnuts** *OR* **Ground Rice**, 2 medium **Eggs**, the soaked Apricots, and finally 1 large **Dessert Apple** washed and cut into small chunks.(No need to peel.) Mix thoroughly, then put into a lined and greased 2 lb Loaf Tin. Spread the top to make sure no fruit is sticking up and bake at 180°C / 160°C Fan / Mark 4 for 45 minutes, or until a skewer inserted into the middle comes out clean.

Leave to cool in tin. Store in fridge after day one (if any left !!)

Caribbean Upside-down Cake

Preparation: 30 minutes
Cooking: 35 minutes

In a *Food Processor* whizz together 1 peeled **Kiwi Fruit**, 3 slices from a tin of **Pineapple Rings** in natural juice and ¼ block **Creamed Coconut**. Grease a round shallow ovenproof dish (about 230 mm / 9" diameter), then spread the fruity coconut purée in the bottom. In the processor (no need to wash in between) whizz together another ¼ block of **Creamed Coconut**, 60 g / 2 oz **Dairy-free Spread** suitable for baking, 2 **Eggs**, 150 g / 5½ oz **Wholemeal Self-Raising Flour** and 100g / 3½ oz **Ground Rice**. Remove the bowl from the base and carefully take out the blades. Now stir in by hand the remaining 5 Pineapple Rings cut into small chunks. You could also add small chunks of a second Kiwi fruit if you like. Spread the cake mix over the purée and bake at 190°C / 170°C Fan / Mark 5 for about 35 minutes, or until evenly browned. The cake floats up on its sticky base. Leave in the dish until just slightly warm, then turn out onto a plate. For a party look, decorate with grated coconut and slivers of pineapple.

Coconut and Banana Loaf

(Gluten, Sugar and Dairy-free)
All kinds of Hawaiian flavours!

Preparation: 20 minutes
Cooking: 50–60 minutes

Gently melt half a block of **Creamed Coconut** in a pan in 140 ml / ¼ pint **hot water**. Heat for a minute or two while stirring all the time but DO NOT OVERHEAT, or it goes too thick. Leave to cool a little, then mash 2 large **ripe Bananas** in a mixing bowl. To these add the melted coconut liquid,150 g / 5 oz **Gluten-free Flour**, 60 g / 2 oz **Ground Rice**, 5 ml / 1 teaspoon **Gluten-free Baking Powder**, ½ teaspoon each of **Cinnamon** and **Nutmeg**, with enough **Pineapple Juice** (add a dash of **Rum** if feeling reckless!) to make a fairly soft battery mix. *(Note: If you use the Rum this may add sugar content to the cake.)* Pour the mixture into a lined greased 1 lb loaf tin and bake at 160°C / 140°C Fan / Mark 3 for 50–60 minutes, or until skewer inserted comes out clean. Cool in tin. *This cake has a close dense texture because of the rice and liquids.*

If the whole loaf will be eaten that day, here's a nice topping: 75 g / 3 oz **Creamed Coconut** dissolved in 2 tablespoons of **hot water**, 1 small **ripe Banana** mashed, finely-grated zest and juice of 1 **Lime** (*or* 1 tablespoon bottled **Lime Juice**). Reserve a little zest to sprinkle on top of the frosting.

Mandarin and Cashew Nut Buns

Preparation: 25 minutes
Cooking: 20–25 minutes

Grease a 12 deep hole bun tin (preferably non-stick), or prepare 8 Cup Cake cases. Pre-heat the oven to 200°C / 180°C Fan / Mark 5.

Drain a 312 g Tin of **Mandarin Oranges in Natural Juice** *but reserve the juice and 8 or 12 intact segments*. In a liquidiser goblet whizz together 90 g / 3 oz **Cashew Nuts** in the reserved orange juice, (made up to 200 ml / 7 fl oz if necessary),the pared rind of half a normal **Orange** and 1 **Banana**. Separate 2 **Medium Eggs** and whisk the whites in a bowl until stiff. Gently stir in the cashew mixture, the egg yolks, 125 g / 4 oz **Wholemeal Self-Raising Flour** with ½ teaspoon of **Cinnamon** or **Nutmeg** and, if liked, 1 tablespoon of crushed **Walnuts** (optional) or walnut meal. Finally fold in the drained mandarin oranges very carefully, so as to keep the air that has been whisked into the egg whites.

Once the mixture is fully blended put a heaped tablespoonful in each bun hole, or divide between the Cup Cake cases. Bake for 8 minutes, then gently press the reserved segments into the top of each of the buns/cup cakes. Cook buns for a further 10–12 minutes, or until gently browned,and until the top of the bun springs back when pressed gently. Cup cakes, being deeper, will need a few minutes more. If any buns are left over, store in the fridge because of the juicy fruit in them. Best eaten warm.

Pear and Chocolate Cake

Preparation: 20 minutes
Cooking: 30–35 minutes

Grease a round flan dish, about 23 cm / 9" in diameter. Drain 1 large tin of **Pear halves in natural juice** and arrange the pears in a circle in the dish, points towards the centre and hollow side downwards. Next mix together 175 g / 6 oz **Dairy-free spread** suitable for baking, 30g / 1 oz **Dark soft brown sugar**, 2 Eggs, 75 g / 3 oz **Ground Almonds**, 5 ml / 1 teaspoon **Almond Essence** 150 g / 5 oz **Wholemeal Self-Raising Flour**, 30 g / 1 oz **Cocoa** and 100 ml / 3½ fl oz mixture of the pear juice and **Red Grape Juice**. (The grape juice adds depth to the scrumptious chocolatey taste, but all pear juice would do.) Spread the cake mixture over the pears carefully, leaving a little of each peeping through, and bake at 160°C / 140°C Fan / Mark 3 for 30–35 minutes. Soon after taking the cake out of the oven, loosen gently round the edge, then leave until only slightly warm and turn onto a plate.(You can then transfer it to another plate to get it the right way up!)

Prune and Apple Squares

Preparation: Soaking time + 15 minutes
Cooking: 30–35 minutes

People often love this cake even if they think they don't like Prunes! You could just not tell them........

*If you've got used to less sweet cakes by now and like a tang, substitute a medium **cooking apple** grated and a large one chunked. The result will be quite a juicy dense cake, but delicious!*

Snip 6 **Prunes** into 3–4 pieces each, depending on size. Soak for 2–3 hours in enough sweet **Pure Apple Juice** to cover. When fruit has soaked line and grease a shallow tin about 200 mm / 8" square. In a mixing bowl combine prunes and juice with 125 g / 4 oz **Dairy-free Spread** suitable for baking, 180 g / 6 oz **Wholemeal Self-Raising Flour**, ½ teaspoon each of **Cinnamon** and **Nutmeg**, 2 **Eggs**, and lastly 1 **Eating Apple** grated and another **Eating Apple** in small chunks. If necessary add a splash of very hot water from the kettle to give a soft but not sloppy consistency.

> ***Note:*** *at this final stage you could add ½ cup of hand-crushed **Bran Flakes** or similar for a bit of crunchy texture. It's a great way to use up the end of a packet!*

Spread the mixture into the prepared tin and bake at 160°C / 140°C Fan / Mark 3 for about 25 minutes, raising the heat to 190°C / 170°C Fan / Mark 5 for another 5–10 minutes at the end to finish browning. Allow to cool in the tin, then cut into squares to serve.

Prune cake

Preparation: Soak time + 20 minutes
Cooking: 30 minutes

This is adapted from the wonderful Cranks recipe book, where it has a topping and appears as 'Sticky Prune Cake.'

Soak 100 g / 3½ oz of **Pitted Prunes** (but not the ready-to-eat kind) in enough boiling water to cover and leave to stand for a few hours, or overnight.

In a basin, whisk together 100 ml / 4 fl oz **Sunflower Oil**, 2 **Eggs** and 30 g / 1 oz **Soft Brown Sugar** (dark is good), until the mixture is fairly thick and creamy. Stir in 150 g / 5 oz **Plain Wholemeal Flour**, ½ teaspoon each of **Mixed Spice** and **Bicarbonate of Soda** and 1 teaspoon each of **Cinnamon** and **Nutmeg**. Beat all well together. Now stir in the prunes, roughly chopped (I use kitchen scissors), and 100 ml / 4 fl oz mixture containing 1 tablespoon **natural soya yoghurt** made up to the quantity with **soya** or **rice 'milk'**.

Pour mixture into a well-greased (lined if you like) 23 cm / 9" square tin, or equivalent round tin if you prefer.

Bake at 180°C / 160°C Fan / Mark 4) for about 30 minutes, until firm to the touch. Leave to cool in the tin.

If you want the topping, it's 1-2-3 of Molasses-Brown Sugar-Soya 'yoghurt' with 'milk', as above, (level tablespoons) melted together with a few drops of vanilla essence and poured hot over the pricked hot cake, leaving it to go very sticky!

Quick Chunky Fruit Loaf

Preparation: Soak time + 20 minutes
Cooking: 45–50 minutes

For this one you don't even need to weigh anything, but you do need to soak the fruit the night before, or at least a couple of hours before you start. It's pretty low on fat and full of fruit.

In a mixing bowl put about 20 pieces of **Large Dried Fruit** (e.g. **Dates**, **Pear**, **Apricots**, **Prunes**, **Figs**) and cut each into 2–3 pieces, according to size. Add enough **Apple Juice** to cover. Leave to soak for 2–3 hours, or overnight. Add 1 tablespoon crushed **Pecan Nuts** (or chopped Almonds or Hazels if you prefer), 1 heaped tablespoon **Dairy-free Spread** suitable for baking, 1 large **Egg** beaten, one 300 ml / half-pint mugful **Wholemeal Flour** *(either Self-Raising, or with 1 teaspoon Baking Powder added)*. Mix all together, adding a little more apple juice or flour, as needed, to give a soft but not runny consistency. Put into a lined and greased 2 lb Loaf Tin, or similar, and bake at 160°C / 140°C Fan / Mark 3 for 45 minutes, or until a skewer comes out clean. If necessary brown at a slightly higher temperature for another 5–10 minutes. Allow to cool in the tin.

Notes